After the Crisis...

SECOND-NATURE SOBRIETY©

K.M.CUSACK

After the Crisis...**SECOND-NATURE SOBRIETY**©

Copyright © 2010 by K.M.CUSACK

Published by SNS Ventures
P.O. Box 4633
Foster City, Ca. 94404
(650) 787-8750
secondnaturesobriety.com

ISBN 978-0-615-43301-1

DEDICATION

This small literary work is not exclusively about recovery, recuperation, or repair, but is equally about restoration and resonance made possible through the revitalization of a Human Spirit and it is dedicated to my best friend and spouse, Margo. I know that I am leaving a famous line from a Tom Cruise movie in the dust ("You complete me.") when I say, "You are my Life Force."

To our children, Colleen and Sean, may your love and trust continue to re-emerge.

To my sisters and brother, thank you for the endless expressions of care and support.

A very large expression of "Thanks" is extended to all who were kind enough to review this material prior to publication. Each of you contributed greatly to the effort in prevention of my condition of Writer's Blindness reaching a terminal stage.

While this work does have a targeted focus area, it contains information that may prove useful to anyone wishing to make a beneficial and sustainable transformation in their life.

Foreword

You're in the right place. You've recognized that the idea of making a change in your life might be a prudent action. Whether you've come to this realization on your own or as a result of informal or formal intervention such as attending a Rehab program, the content in this book may prove useful in achieving your targeted goal.

This is one point in your life where it really *is* All About You. The choice that you have before you is fundamental and the result of your selection can be foundational and profound.

Achieving positive Foundational Change will result in a sensation you may not have experienced in quite a while. It's called "Happiness" and it is sustained by Authenticity.

My goal was to achieve a state of Natural Sobriety. I wanted to live without constant focus on abstinence and avoidance in favor of living with authenticity and comfortable confidence. I made effective choices along the way and applied appropriate effort during the Change Process. The result has not been limited to recovery from addiction, but has been expanded to include a rediscovery of personal characteristics which now sustain an approach to living I had previously regarded as simply unachievable.

This small book has been created with the hope that you similarly accomplish your goal.

Table of Contents

THE WAKEUP CALL

"Do you remember how you got here?"

"Do you remember what happened before the ambulance arrived?"

"Do you know where you are right now?

"Do you remember....?"

I had just regained a fuzzy degree of consciousness when the I. C. U. resident started posing the questions. "No", "no", and "no" were probably my answers, but I don't really recall.

Eventually, I learned about the 14-day stay in the Unit which included a 6-day forced coma with machines breathing for me and feeding me through some network of tubes. They didn't tell me about the "Depends" I had to wear, though. I guess some dignity is better than none. I was almost happy when I was told that memory loss was a common recovery symptom for seizure patients.

Passing out from drinking too much wasn't new to me. In fact, I had achieved a high level of proficiency with that step in the Self-Abuse process. What *was* new was passing out from *not drinking*. This was "Ah Hah" material!

"How could this happen?"

"What did I do to deserve this?"

"Why did this happen to me?

Those were the questions I was asking. My answer ... "Guess what, Champ?"
"You're a world-class alcoholic. You've finally made it to the Big Time."

My "crisis" had arrived...or so I thought...

I made it home on extremely shaky legs, both physically and psychologically. Don't bother wondering how my spirit was doing. I didn't protest when, a few days later, I was on my way to a Rehab facility in Oakland. "Whoopee, I'm goin' on vacation." Somebody had even packed a bag for me. I was about to start adding a few more bucks to the medical bills which, by now, were well over $225,000. (Don't ask me to vote "yes" for any Insurance Reform.)

When I next saw the light of day, I had finished the inpatient phase and was on my way home. My outpatient phase would begin the next day and I'd be done in 20. "Isn't sobriety a wonderful thing?", I thought. "I felt *exactly* this way the *last time* I came out of Rehab." I thought they had done such a good job at this most recent facility, they *must* have cured me. I would be abstinent for about six months before I began testing that assumption.

After three or four months of "testing" had passed, I had the owners of at least three liquor stores considering expansion. I was convinced they didn't know I had "a problem" since I *only* visited one of them every three days. And I never missed a visit.

When my wife's foot was once more put down for "the last time", I reduced my consumption significantly. This delayed my resulting seizure for a few days and then it was off to the hospital *again.* You may find this to be absolutely incredible, but, *I Wasn't Done Yet.*

Within a few days of my release, I was drinking while taking Librium. I'll just bet it's a real mystery for you trying to figure out where I wound up.

I've "graduated" so many times from Rehab, I should get frequent flyer miles.

I share all of this "history" and the material that follows for a number of reasons;

- I want you to be aware that the person who assembled the following material has "creds".

- I truly hope the material helps you in some way.

- There are alternatives to the 12-Step approach that you should get exposure to.

- A "One Size Fits All" approach to Natural Abstinence has absolutely no logic to support it.

- I believe that your exercise of Choice is the most important step you can take toward creating the freedom you deserve.

Your Commitment, Attitude, and Knowledge can function as tools that can reap enormous benefits for you and others in your life. With the addition of time and effort, you'll soon be on your way toward creating...

SECOND-NATURE SOBRIETY

WHAT NOW?

You've done your inpatient/outpatient 10, 30, 60, or 90-day "dryout and rehab" stint. Your counselor congratulated you on your achievement, handed you the standard A.A. pamphlet, and wished you well. This may not have been your first experience with this situation and you know that the odds are against you that it will be your last.

Your "crisis" that precipitated program enrollment may have ranged in severity from someone in your life suggesting "you may have a problem" to the higher extreme of having your participation mandated by a judge as part of your plea-bargain for the involuntary manslaughter charge you face, for your legal separation agreement, or for your bankruptcy protection filing. Your medical condition may have also played a role.

Whatever occurred in your world that resulted in program participation will now serve as the basis for your going-forward decision about whether to continue with this newly found or rediscovered State of Abstinence. On one hand, you may try to rationalize, minimize, and trivialize the behavior(s) or event(s) that preceded your participation. You may feel that you've served your time and done your "Penance." After all, this is *You* we're talking about here and, *You're Special*, right? On the other hand, you may be facing a "Life is Over" kind of situation and you feel hopeless since all prior attempts at abstinence failed. Why bother now?

If either of the two mindsets described above belong to you, let's just wish each other well, say, "Happy Trails", and go about our respective lives.

However, if you've arrived at the conclusion that you need to continue to change, then the material on the following pages may help you along. If you'd rather not live a life dominated by substance abuse or impulsive, harmful behavior, it is not only *possible* to do so, it *can become* **Second-Nature**.

As a recent program graduate, you've been exposed to the Great Debate as to whether Alcoholism is a disease. You've been educated regarding the addictive characteristics of other substances and behaviors. You've been equipped with all kinds of knowledge about how to avoid slips and relapses. You've started to abandon the "old haunts" and stopped hanging out with the "old crowd". You've even heard that being abstinent isn't that difficult; it's the *living* part that's hard. Congratulations!...you now have a firm foundation for living a Life of Avoidance.

Here you are, newly- referred to a 12 Step program of some type, expecting revelation and rebirth. You intend to follow the prescribed route to a life free of addiction. You'll find a sponsor to guide you through The Steps. If you remain with the program for a year, you will be counted among the 5% of newcomers who do so after that period of time has elapsed. You might come to realize that the Program is dominating your free time and that your life has become "meetingful" rather than "meaningful".

Where you once had a submissive relationship with a substance or a behavior, you now have one with a Program that provides "suggestions" for leading your life. Should you experience a slip or a relapse along the way, it's back to Step 1 and all periods of abstinence are considered null and void. Could it be that you subconsciously rebelled against the dominating approach? Would you still be abstinent if *you* made the style-of-life decisions? Where would you be now if *you* controlled the Program? Would you be a practitioner of Positive Life Skills or living a Life of Avoidance?

If you'd prefer a more balanced approach to living, an approach that doesn't involve fanatical focus on abstinence, an approach that considers sobriety to be a natural life-choice and not the result of a self-imposed deprivation, then I encourage you to learn more. As you explore the content of these pages, look for what you feel will work for you. Please leave your cynicism at the door. Put aside your biases, prejudices, and preconceived notions. Review the material with an open, blank-slate frame of mind.

Take some nuggets, not the whole mine. This was the approach I used in researching all of the excellent sources listed at the end of this work. Continue your exploration with those sources as well. Many are found at your local library where you're also likely to have free internet access.

Lastly, and as a former, transplanted New Yorker, if someone has you thinking, "*I'm Powerless.*", then tell'em, "*fuggedaboudit*". What we all have is *Potential* and the front *halfadat* word is a synonym for *Power*. Acknowledging our potential generates genuine confidence toward any personal transformation effort.

You've had your crisis and recuperation. Now, it's time…*After the Crisis…*

SECOND-NATURE SOBRIETY

"No problem can be solved from the same level of consciousness that created it." - Albert Einstein

THE BATTLE WITHIN

One evening, an old Cherokee gazed at his grandson and recognized that the boy had a battle going on inside himself.

He said, "My son, the battle within you is between two wolves.

"One wolf is evil and is filled with anger, envy, sorrow, regret, greed, arrogance, self-pity, guilt, resentment, inferiority, lies, false pride, superiority, and ego."

"The other wolf is good and is filled with joy, peace, love, hope, serenity, humility, kindness, benevolence, empathy, generosity, truth, compassion, and faith."

The grandson thought about this for a while and then asked his grandfather, "Which wolf wins?"

The old Cherokee replied, "The one you feed."

IT'S ALL ABOUT CHANGE

The preceding quote and the Wolf story serve as simple, yet effective, examples of what the process of achieving SECOND-NATURE SOBRIETY involves and where your mindset needs to be. It is simply about making a Change and creating your supporting Internal Culture. Keeping the process simple is what the upcoming material is all about. The amount of personal effort you apply will determine your level of success.

The effort becomes worthwhile when you realize that you've *stopped even thinking* about your former object of addiction and your choice to be abstinent has evolved into a natural personal trait. Being sober has become just another facet of your personality and your character. It has become **Second-Nature**.

There is a severe education gap that exists following your physical recuperation and your introduction, or reintroduction, to the "Sober World" that causes a slew of negative feelings and barriers to successful change that need to be resolved. Among the primary issues needing to be addressed is learning about the Change Process itself, what makes it successful, and, most importantly, what it takes to make the change *naturally sustainable*. After that, we'll look at the other equally important issues you're likely wrestling with at the moment such as Self-Esteem, Shame & Guilt, and Attitude. The fact that the outcome we're seeking with these and other issues is Foundational Change requires a knowledge of the process involved and not just a list of helpful "tips". Achieving a Foundational Change is the outcome of practiced skills. A lack of success in this area may be one of the most significant contributors to the slips and relapses that commonly occur in the Rehabilitation arena.

During your "using days", you operated within the mindset of a Consequential Victim with no inclination or perceived necessity to make a change. Your "crisis" had yet to arrive and your personal Pleasure Palace had not yet started to crumble. Ask yourself now if you're ready to commit to a Foundational Change. If you have even a tinge of doubt, don't bother with the effort. You'll only slip or relapse your way back to whatever source of artificial euphoria led you to the point of crisis.

Attempting Foundational Change without a firm commitment coupled with practiced skills is nothing but a formula for frustration and failure.

"But I don't want to take a test..."

It's a good idea to start with a brief assessment of your Reaction to Change in general. All you need is a blank piece of paper, a pen or pencil, and someone to keep time for you. This will take less than 5 minutes and you should <u>pay special attention to your feelings</u> from this point forward.

Fold the paper in half lengthwise or draw a line down the middle. Place the pen or pencil in whichever hand you normally write with. Choose which side of the paper you will write on and ask your partner to time you for 30 seconds. When your partner says, "GO", begin printing your name. Print it as many times as you can until your partner says, "STOP".

Now put the pen or pencil in your other hand and ask your partner to time you for 60 seconds. When your partner says, "GO", begin printing your name on the blank side of the paper. Print it as many times as you can until you hear, "STOP".

Let's review what some of your most likely feelings were in parts one and two. (These feelings would also have been amplified if this exercise were conducted in a group setting due to some public performance issues that are common to many of us.)

From the point at which you learned what was needed for this little exercise, your pulse rate may have quickened, you may have been annoyed that you were being "assessed", or maybe you just didn't like having your reading interrupted to perform a task you can do *without even thinking about it*. On the other hand, you may have reserved judgment about how you felt until you learned more about the proposed task.

What did you feel when you learned that you were going to use your other hand for step 2? Were you anxious and uncertain about your ability to perform a familiar task using unfamiliar methods? Did you get frustrated and impatient with your lack of success? How could you only produce about half the amount of printed names that you were able to produce in step 1 when you were given twice the amount of time in step 2? Were you filled with self-doubt? Did you give up trying?

This brief exercise points out some of the possible reactions you may have when you're faced with the necessity and/or desire to change something in your life, but you lack the practiced skills to experience consistent success. It also points out the frustration caused when trying to do something differently without having learned the methods needed to develop the appropriate skills.

> **"That a man can change himself…and master his own destiny is the conclusion of every mind who is wide awake to the power of right thought."**
> - Christian D. Larsen (1866-1954)

MINDSETS of CHANGE

In the name-printing exercise, you had a brief and basic exposure to your particular reaction to change. Your reaction was generated by a mindset developed through experiences you've previously had when dealing with change. Your mindset predetermines your Changeability. The mindsets can be generally categorized as;

VICTIM – SURVIVOR – THRIVER

and they should be viewed as phases or as a continuum. You can move from left to right or from right to left. You can feel you are completely in one category (you're not), have a foot in each of two (more likely), or be spread among all three (most likely).

What is important and what will lead to your success in dealing with change, is that you are aware of your positioning and then take steps to respond accordingly. You can re-label the categories to suit your targeted development needs;

VICTIM – SURVIVOR – THRIVER

DENIAL - ACCEPTANCE - RESPONSIBILITY

ADDICTION – RECUPERATION – SOBRIETY

Sobriety is the result of change. If you have addiction issues, you also have change issues. Focusing on this fact is a start toward the attainment of **SECOND-NATURE SOBRIETY**.

The reason why Sobriety may feel strange at the moment is that it represents a change in your personal, internal culture. Your internal culture is the breeding ground for your mindset. When the need for a change comes along, your internal culture needs to be accepting and supporting of it.

Any general resistance to change is normally driven by Ego and a distorted Self-Image. Change is like trying on some new clothes. Ultimately, we don't like change because it makes our "BUT" look too big.

All successful Foundational Change requires an accepting and supportive culture in order for the effort to be sustainable.

BARRIERS TO CHANGE

If we had a few hours to create a list of specifics for this topic, it probably wouldn't be enough time. It's a safe bet that Procrastination, Stubbornness, Denial, Anger, and Ego would be on it along with many, many others. Rather than listing all of the specifics, a better approach may be to list general areas that produce those specifics. You can then create a list that is tailored to you for your own consideration.

<u>Failing to see the Need</u>

I'm sure you've heard the saying, "Ignorance is Bliss". How often have you done the same thing repeatedly and expected a different result? That defines Insanity as well as Ignorance. What causes the failure to recognize that a change needs to be made?

In response to that question, I have a sudden image in my mind of Dana Carvey's character from Saturday Night Live, *The Church Lady*, saying, "*Could it be SATIN?*"

Actually, what's at work here is more likely to be Blind Ego. "*Isn't that Special?*"

Ignorance has been described as "the inability to see the true nature of things".

Not Knowing and Understanding Yourself

Conducting a thorough, honest, and accurate assessment of your strengths and areas needing improvement is an absolute necessity in order to make a successful change. Don't ignore an opportunity to seek input from trusted others in your life for this process.

There is an excellent website, Authentic Happiness, that features the work of Dr. Martin Seligman, Director - University of Pennsylvania Positive Psychology Center. Here, you can take a survey of your VIA Character Strengths and learn which of 24 Strengths are among your top 5.

Has it been a while since they were last exercised? Are they as strong and as active as they once were? Look for other Strengths that may need some attention as well since they will support your change to Second Nature Sobriety. Take the tests again in six months to see if things have changed. Participating in some of the other available surveys will help you to fill other gaps about self-knowledge you're interested in pursuing.

More importantly, this website is a source of information that can help you construct a lifestyle that is ultimately founded on Authenticity rather than a lifestyle based on Avoidance i.e., living with apprehension and fear of the future.

Stop Looking Forward to the Past

Nothing puts an end to a Change Effort faster than romancing the "old days". Any fondness you may have for them is likely to be based on delusion and illusion. Unless you *really do* want to repeat the past, put an end to this useless behavior. What <u>has been</u> and what <u>might have been</u> always bring you back to <u>what is</u>.

Not Knowing What to Change

The previous survey of your Strengths can be viewed in different ways.

You can certainly view the survey results as being verification of your self-perception, but they can also be viewed as a source of illumination aimed at your self-deception.

Ask yourself, "Do my actions and behavior serve as examples of my Strengths?" "Under what circumstances and situations does this occur?" More importantly ask, "How often does this happen?"

If your answer to that last question is, "Not as often as it used to.", you may begin to gain some insight as to what needs to change. As the frequency rate of substance abuse or undesirable behavior increased in your life, your natural or Second-Nature Strengths started to falter. They gradually gave way to a supporting cast of characteristics which can tactfully be called "Areas for Improvement. In those circumstances, your perceived "Strengths" became passive while your "Areas for Improvement" evolved to become your current strengths. Putting it more bluntly, you're looking at "I Used to Be" and "Where I'm At".

Your "Areas for Improvement" are those areas that have gradually received most of your attention and exercise for quite a while, aren't they? As a result, they are now (unfortunately) among the stronger characteristics supporting not only substance abuse and undesirable behavior, but your general approach to living. This should give you some clarity regarding your level of Denial and Self-Deception.

Applying misdirected effort while you're attempting Change doesn't get you anywhere other than where you're at. Focus on what is *supporting* the behavior.

Not Knowing How to Change

Do you know someone in your life that has taken a few Self-Improvement classes or maybe purchased the latest Diet book? As they're telling you all about the benefits, you're realizing that nothing has changed. They've collected *information* about Change, they *learned* about Change, they may have *practiced* the Change, but they haven't *adopted* the Change.

We don't change through the process of Education. We don't change through the process of Application. We don't change through the process of Incorporation, either.

We change through the process of Adoption. We change when we make a choice to allow a personal characteristic to become **Second-Nature**.

Not Maintaining the "New Way"

Even the strongest muscles need exercise or they will eventually atrophy. What is it that falls by the wayside causing us to fail in the maintenance of a change in our lives? Are there multiple causes? A big cause might be that our Impulsiveness has grown stronger than our Patience over time or that our focus is placed on Gratification rather than Gratitude.

Our tendency toward Impulsiveness can be reduced through an increase in the strength of Mindfulness and Awareness. These are two essential skills that also need to be developed in order to hear that inner voice we sometimes hear saying, "The other way wasn't really *that* bad. Come on back…"

Failing to Transition the "New" to "Normal"

If the change in your life continues to be an isolated subject of attention, it will never become integrated within your personal "fabric". It will always be something you're "working on" and will never become a part of the Normal You. Why can't you get comfortable with it? Wouldn't life be easier if the change evolved into a Second-Nature characteristic?

You can't get comfortable with the change since your current "cast" of supporting personality characteristics is eagerly awaiting your slip, your relapse, or the complete abandonment of the Change Effort.

Commit to the fact that "New" will become Second-Nature and that the "Old" no longer has influence. You have the power of Choice available for you now. Choice is what will awaken your star players; your Core Strengths.

Failing to Own the Change

Putting some*one* or some*thing* in charge of the change means having no responsibility for the outcome, but you've become accustomed to operating that way, right? You're still ready to play the Blame Game.

What's holding you back from making this yours? Do you really think Meeting Attendance and Avoidance are going to do it for you all by themselves? All of the professional counseling in the world won't do it either unless another element is brought into the mix.

What may be holding you back is lack of Ownership of Change derived from Choice. By choosing to make the change *yours*, you assume Ownership and Responsibility for the outcome. Your current supporting "cast" of personality characteristics may not like this approach, but you'll soon be evicting them anyway. <u>Foundational Change is not rented or loaned; it is owned.</u>

Now… *Take Five* in your "Happy Place". We'll next be looking at approaches to ease you along in the Change Process.

FACILITATING CHANGE

It may seem ironic, but some of the very same factors that produce Resistance to Change (Ego and Individuality) also serve as factors that produce Enthusiasm for Change. In addition, the Stubbornness, Procrastination, etc., which supported Resistance, now need to be supplanted by Commitment and Action; two essential ingredients in the recipe for Successful Change. Only full amounts of both should be added to the mix.

<u>Create a Vision</u>

Picture yourself in the not-too-distant future operating with recently revitalized personal strengths such as Honesty and Integrity. Does this person behave like someone you once were? Having a realistic vision of what the change will accomplish provides a motivating incentive for action and ownership.

<u>You are Worthy</u>

It's easy to say, "Forget the actions of the Past." It takes significant personal effort to get there, and you may need a pro to help you in the process of "Letting Go", but it will be worth it to shed the ton (or more) of guilt you've been schlepping along since you most recently gained some clarity and cringed (a lot). You can't make an effective transition to a new way of life until issues from the past are addressed and, hopefully, resolved. Repair what you're able to, keep the personal flogging at a minimum, and move forward. There's some good to be accomplished in your future and acknowledging that fact will likely help you in dealing with any tenacious past issues. *You are definitely worth the effort.*

Admittedly, I still struggle with the Mountain of Misery my behavior has created over the years. At times I wish I could just put an Expiration Date on it, but I'm not made that way.

However, I'm finding that Misery expires gradually for me as I develop more Authenticity in my life. Eventually, I hope my Moral Value Scale tilts more from the weight of the resulting grains of Gratitude than from the rocks of Remorse.

I'm gradually developing an Attitude of Gratitude for Life's Latitude.

<u>Don't Play the Blame Game</u>

Mark Twain opened his one-man shows by saying,

"Nothing needs reforming…so much as other people's habits."

Some folks almost achieve the professional level with this activity and seem to outdo Houdini in the process as they try to escape responsibility for their actions. Point your finger at someone or something for this last time and notice how many of your fingers are clenched and pointing right back at you.

The Power of Choice

I included mention of Choice in the previous section as having a role for knocking down Barriers to Change, but it also deserves to be highlighted as a Facilitator of Change for the role it plays as a stimulator of creativity and freedom.

Choice can send us on a path to reconnect with our Core Strengths. Availability of choice causes us to apply creativity to our approaches toward change. The freedom generated by choice draws us toward what we know will be beneficial.

I had the fortunate opportunity to have a counselor during one of my experiences at an area Rehab unit who took the time to express her opinion regarding the role that Choice plays in the Recovery Process. I owe her a debt of gratitude for opening my eyes. From her I learned that Foundational Change cannot be achieved in the absence of Choice. Thanks, Janice.

Choice strengthens your level of commitment and produces a level of personal performance that you may currently consider to be unrecoverable or even unachievable. Every time you make a choice to repeat that performance level, your Core Strength approaches **Second-Nature** status.

Choice, coupled with Confident Confrontation, is one of the main elements of *Personal Power* we have at our disposal to create and sustain a change in our lives. We can actually *choose* the Attitude and Behavior needed to elevate a change to the level of **Second-Nature**.

Eliminate Falsehood

Telling a few lies to cover our tracks tends to chip away at our Core Strengths. What happens to our Core Strengths as we increase the level of deception and become Masters of Manipulation (or so we thought)? The energy and effort expended to maintain a false identity actually strengthened our ability to devalue ourselves as we pursued the substance or behavior that increasingly dominated our lives. That application of energy and effort needs to be refocused in support of the Change Effort.

Set Incremental Goals

"Too much too soon" always seems to be a recipe for failure and it reinforces our devalued self-image. Change in comfortable amounts at a comfortable pace that works for you. Experience success incrementally and you're likely to accomplish more with manageable effort. The change will be *sustainable* as a result.

Celebrate Success

Learn new ways to celebrate success other than by ingesting substances or engaging in inappropriate behavior that can cause harm. Be especially wary about jumping on the Sugarland Express. You'll only wind up joining my class-action lawsuit against the local drycleaner for maliciously shrinking clothes.

Leverage Your Strengths

The exercise of one Core Strength can have a rippling effect, i.e., Practicing Honesty impacts your Integrity. Practicing Humility impacts Patience. The Process of Change is made a bit easier knowing that your effort in one area goes a long way.

<u>Patience, Patience, and more Patience</u>

Aren't you just a little tired of Impulse, Impulse, and more Impulse? You grew accustomed to Action Without Thought, right?

Now it's time to reintroduce Patience. It will prove to be one of your most valued assets as you move through the Change Process. From Patience, you will develop the level of "Guardfullness" required to silence the voice you may sometimes hear saying, "You're fine ... Come on back…"

<u>Practice, Practice, and more Practice</u>

To make a change part of your personal "fabric", it must be repeated many times in order for it to evolve into a natural behavior. This repetitive action also decreases the likelihood that we will revert to our "old ways" or succumb to even the slightest temptation to reactivate past habits. As the change evolves into habit, it is nearing **Second-Nature** status.

(I purposely omitted the **Desire to Change** from the preceding list since I assumed you were familiar with the old joke regarding the number of shrinks it takes to change a light bulb ... one, but the light bulb has to want to change.)

Having the **Desire to Change** is certainly essential and we also know the importance of developing a personal Internal Culture that is accepting and supportive of Change. However, we won't get very far in the process if we fail to acknowledge the need to address elements in our lives that continue to be the source of current hesitancy and self-doubt. I'm referring to the issues of **Self-Esteem, Shame & Guilt**, and **Attitude** and these are the areas we will next review.

THREE ADDITIONAL PRIMARY
ISSUES

At the beginning of the preceding sections, I introduced **Knowledge about the Process of Change** as being among the primary issues needing to be addressed in order to make a Foundational Transformation leading to the development of **Second-Nature Sobriety** as a Core Strength.

Well, just like those infomercials on TV that we all know and love...Wait, there's more. Yes, that's right. You not only get the special information about Change, but we're including our premium package as well which includes a look at **Self-Esteem**, **Shame & Guilt**, and **Attitude**. As an added bonus, Shipping and Handling are free!

<u>SELF-ESTEEM</u>

Feelings of inferiority, incompetence, worthlessness, and resentment are classic characteristics of someone with low self-esteem. The inability to make a change depends on their presence. We wouldn't be self-defeating without them.

Our whole culture of Denial exists because of them. These feelings help to fuel our self-deception and they represent the power behind our ability to recycle shame and guilt, to repeat unproductive behavior, to live with self-disrespect, and to think it's all "Normal". Why don't we all break out into a rousing rendition of, "1 Gotta Be Me", right about now?

Developed by Nathaniel Branden, PH.D., the **"Six Pillars of Self-Esteem"** could serve as a blueprint for self-reconstruction and as a guide toward achieving a far more positive self-image. He describes Self-Esteem as "the experience of being competent to cope with the basic challenges of life and being worthy of happiness."

Dr. Branden's "Six Pillars" include;

Living Consciously: Paying attention to information and feedback about needs and goals ... facing facts that might be uncomfortable or threatening ... refusing to wander through life in a self-induced mental fog.

Self-Acceptance: Being willing to experience whatever we truly think, feel, or do, even if we don't always like it ... facing our mistakes and learning from them.

Self-Responsibility: Establishing a sense of control over our lives by realizing we are responsible for our choices and actions at every level...the achievement of our goals ... our happiness ... our values.

Self-Assertiveness: The willingness to express appropriately our thoughts, values, and feelings...to stand up for ourselves ... to speak and act from our deepest convictions.

Living Purposely: Setting goals and working to achieve them, rather than living at the mercy of chance and outside forces ... developing self-discipline.

Integrity: The integration of our behavior with our ideals, convictions, standards, and beliefs ... acting in congruence with what we believe is right.

While Dr. Branden feels that "self-esteem is a necessary condition of well-being, it is not the only one." He cautions that it won't make life problem-free. He adds, "Self-Esteem requires us to listen to and respect our own sensations, insights, intuition, and perspective."
Dr. Branden concludes, "For all of us, developing the pillars of self-esteem is a life-long, and worthy, challenge rewarded with Authentic Happiness."

SHAME & GUILT

In the book, "Healing the Shame that Binds You", the author, John Bradshaw, distinguishes the Healthy and Toxic forms of Shame and Guilt;

Healthy Shame is the psychological ground to our Humility.
Toxic Shame is about being flawed as a human being. It is about hopelessness.
(Do you recall when you last experienced either or both of these states?)

Healthy Guilt is the core of our central conscience.
Toxic Guilt is about carrying the world on your shoulders. It is about having to be perfect for the sake of all others. One failure is a complete, life-ending failure.

(Do you recall when you last experienced either or both of these states?)

Bradshaw continues, "Toxic Shame is experienced as the all-pervasive sense that I am flawed and defective as a human being. It becomes a core identity. It gives you a sense of worthlessness, a sense of failing and falling short as a human being. It guards us against exposing ourselves to ourselves, preventing us from living *Authentically*."

"We become the object of our own contempt, an object that can't be trusted. Toxic Shame is the feeling of being isolated and alone in a complete sense. A shame-based person is haunted by a sense of absence and emptiness. It is easily confused with guilt."

He writes, "Neurotic Shame is the root and fuel of all compulsive/addictive behaviors. A definition of compulsive/addictive behavior is 'a pathological relationship to any mood-altering experience that has life-damaging consequences'."

"Addicts can't love themselves. They are an object of scorn to themselves. The deep internalized shame gives rise to distorted thinking. The distorted thinking causes the belief that more self-indulgent behavior will relieve it."

"The motivation in any addiction is the belief that one is a flawed person. The addictive activity creates negative consequences which create more shame. The new shame fuels the Cycle of Addiction which, in turn, fuels the Cycle of Shame."

It seems that we engage in the activity to solve the problems caused by the activity. Great! And we thought nobody knew us a well as we knew ourselves...

Mr. Bradshaw offers a way out of the Toxic Shame by first urging that we "come out of hiding." One way to accomplish this is to find a group you trust enough to achieve comfortable acceptance, not only of you, but of your situation and your desire to change. Mr. Bradshaw has personal justification for his endorsement of A.A., but within my material, you'll be given exposure to other possible sources for your consideration such as LifeRing.

ATTITUDE

"Human beings, by changing the inner attitudes of their minds, can change the outer aspects of their lives."
-William James (1842-1910)

"My life has been full of terrible misfortunes, most of which never happened."
- M.E. DeMontaigne (1592)

Bessie is getting ready for a trip to Rome with her husband, Biff, and decides to pay a visit to Wanda, her hairdresser. She wants her hair to look extra special since the trip is in celebration of their 30th wedding anniversary.

As she settled into the chair, Bessie excitedly shared the news about the trip with Wanda who said, "Rome? Why would anyone wanna go there? I hear it's crowded, dirty, and filled with nothin' but Italians. How ya gettin' there?"

"We're flying on Olympic Airlines", Bessie said. "They had a really good deal available."

"Olympic!", said Wanda. "Why you flyin' them? I hear they're goin' broke, got ugly flight attendants, and are never on time. Where're ya stayin'?"

"We found a romantic hotel called, "*Amore*", just outside of the city.", said Bessie.

Wanda replied, "I've heard about the place. They got really small rooms, no views, and only one bathroom. You plannin' on seein' anything over there?"
"We'd really like to see the Vatican and, hopefully, the Pope", said Bessie.

"Fat chance", said Wanda, "I hear the Vatican's only open Tuesdays and about a half a million people try to get in at the same time. Good luck with that."

Two weeks later, Bessie returns for another hair appointment and Wanda said, "I bet you're glad to be back. The trip was a disaster, right?"

"Actually, it was just the opposite.", said Bessie. "The flight on Olympic was oversold so they had to put us in First Class. The flight attendants were former magazine models and we arrived ahead of schedule. The city was fabulous and incredibly clean. Did you know most Italians take vacation themselves at this time of year? We felt like the city was all ours."

"Well, I bet that hotel was awful, right?", said Wanda.

"You won't believe this!", said Bessie. "They renovated it last year and to help celebrate our anniversary, they put us in their best suite with spectacular views for the regular room price and gave us complimentary room service every morning and afternoon. Now, that's what I call, Amore!"

"Well, you never saw the Vatican, right?" said Wanda.

"Oh, that was the best part.", Bessie said. "The Swiss Guard on duty pulled us aside after we told him about our Anniversary and he told us how much the Pope likes to meet people celebrating such happy events."

"We were escorted to a private audience with the Pope. He entered the room, greeted both of us and then said, "Bessie, I have to ask…Who screwed up your hair ?"

*****

I suppose, at times, we all have the capability to be like Wanda, living with a self-fulfilling negative approach to life. We don't set our sights very high in order to meet our low expectations and the results we get are right on target. If we recycle that approach, we'll never have to confront Happiness which then seems unachievable for us, anyway. Instead, we resort to the pursuit of manufactured Pleasure which results in temporary euphoria. We actually hide from Happiness by choosing a Negative Attitude.

By the way, do you think Bessie felt pleasure, happiness, or both when she told Wanda about her trip and passed along the Papal comment about her hair? It's amazing what a good "dig" can produce.

Attitude can change a roadblock into an opportunity and it can fill the "half-empty" glass. The right Attitude can help you navigate the psychological "minefields" that lay along the abstinence path before "slips" and "relapses" occur. These "minefields" are created by a malicious subconscious that produces that voice saying, "You're fine ... Come on back... ". An Inattentive Attitude will not recognize the "minefield" or acknowledge the voice and we then respond to what seems like an imperceptible impulse. How often does the explanation for a slip include, "I don't know *why* it happened. It just *did*."?

Attentive Attitude, reinforced by commitment, passion, knowledge, and action working together, consciously and subconsciously, will make **Second-Nature Sobriety** a reality. You *will* have successful confrontations with your former addictive nemesis and you *will* come to the realization that you no longer perceive it as having any power, influence, or desirability. You have made the *Choice* to remove it from your existence. You may have even used the approach of a 5-year old and said, "You're not the boss of me!"

Your Attitude should not include fear of the future. Envisioning yourself 48, 72, and 96 hours or more in the future will make your choice to adopt Sobriety as a Core Strength stronger and easier to maintain and sustain. Your Attitude can serve as your "vision engine" and will energize your enthusiasm, your concerted effort, your general morale, and your desire to thrive in the midst of change. Living in 24-hour segments is a cornerstone of a Life of Avoidance, a life of "I Can't" and is ultimately self-limiting. In today's world, it seems thoroughly self-defeating. You may as well audition for a role next to Bill Murray when the sequel to "GROUNDHOG DAY" starts casting. You'll certainly have the experience for it.

Which comes first ... Attitude or Behavior?

Our Attitude has a direct impact on our Behavior, but isn't the opposite true as well?

I believe our Attitude drives and sustains our Behavior and that our Behavior reinforces our Attitude. (Then again, I'm still working on the chicken or the egg thing, too.)

We've reached a point where we know something has to change in the way we conduct ourselves. We've explored the Change Process, what potentially stands in the way, and what can help us along in that effort. We've addressed Self-Esteem, Shame & Guilt, and Attitude.

Before moving forward to the next sections, I want to point out that this material you're reading isn't just about recovery, rehabilitation, or recuperation. It is about rediscovery, restoration, and revitalization of Core Strengths that support a positive and authentic Human Spirit. These Strengths are customized by our individual natures, but are common to us all in a more general sense. Through the active practice of Addiction, they become warped or even supplanted. I believe it is the reason why constant personal internal conflict is merged with the misery of Addiction.

If you're looking for an example of this personal internal conflict, just think back to the last time you said,

"I must have been out of my mind. I don't know *what* I was thinking. It wasn't me."

If you're really tired of saying those things and would like to continue to pursue Foundational Change, then these next sections may prove useful.

Let's have a look at **Honesty**, **Commitment**, **Ethics**, and **Integrity**.

RELENTLESS SELF-HONESTY

"Honesty is the cornerstone of all success, without which confidence and ability to perform shall cease to exist." - Mary Kay Ash

"Honesty is the first chapter in the book of Wisdom." - Thomas Jefferson

If there is one area in the Change Effort that represents Mt. Everest, this is it. What will become our new positive attitude, commitment, patience, gratitude, awareness, choice, and our Second-Nature Sobriety are directly impacted by the relentless presence of Self-Honesty. In order to achieve our targeted change, there needs to be a 180-degree shift in our self-perception.

An addictive lifestyle requires a base or a foundation of deceit, denial, betrayal, delusion and general dishonesty that takes an enormous amount of time and energy to construct and maintain. We live with a self-created False

Identity with its own set of Ethics. The longer this lifestyle is practiced, the larger the pile of lies becomes. It seems insurmountable at times and it reinforces our need to isolate since we feel there's no way around it or over it. Negative self-rationalization wins every time.

When the choice has been made to finally put an end to Addiction, make use of the time and energy formally used to support negative pursuits and focus it on developing relentless Self-Honesty. You may not have positive reactions to the word "relentless" as it can bring to mind images of a whiny two-year old or a nagging mother-in-law. In the case of Self-Honesty, though, it can bring about a change in your Self-Image that is amazingly liberating. Imagine the weight of the pile of lies being lifted from your shoulders, but that's only a first step. Each time you exercise Self-Honesty, you re-fortify other Core Strengths. This tendency toward relentless Self-Honesty becomes self-sustaining as you experience more instances of authentic happiness. You may even begin to feel happy for what seems to be no reason. That is one of the ultimate benefits of relentless Self-Honesty.

Mindset Change

False Identity – True Self Awareness – Authentic You

"What they don't know…"
Maybe it might be more accurate to say, "If I don't provide, I won't have to hide." Lying through omission is not just a little white lie. It is outright Deceit. If it is practiced often enough, it just gets added to the ever-growing bag of tricks used to support addictive behavior. We give it justification by presenting it with the altruistic reasoning that

it is for the protection of others when, in fact, it is entirely self-serving. The main allure of it is the convenience factor and the complete lack of effort required in its application.

"There's no way they can prove it…"
Our ability to avoid the truth becomes so pervasive over time that we will use it in response to even the most mundane inquiries rather than marring our consistency through the occasional exercise of honesty. If it can't be verified, we automatically lie in support of our Denial abilities.

Some examples:

"Did you pick up such-and-such at the store like I asked?"
"They were out of them." (You never went)

"Did you make an appointment for the car?"
"Yeah, yeah." (You didn't)

"Did you feed the fish?"
"Of course." (Two days ago)

Honesty is a hallmark of Authenticity. Addicts instinctively and impulsively lie. Addiction crushes our instinct to be honest except when we have no deceitful alternative. Abstinence hopefully makes us aware of this tendency and makes us conscious of it when we try to revert to it. Our increasing mental clarity should make us more mindful of this characteristic. General Mindfulness Practices will eventually tame, diminish, and, ultimately, erase this tendency. The path will then be clear for the emergence of Authenticity. You may actually stop saying, "I don't know why it happened. It just happened."

"No one will ever know…"

As you continue the exercise of Self-Honesty, you will begin to notice a change in your interactions with people in your lives (and with yourself, as well). Those closest to you who have lost trust in you will gradually begin to recognize that something has changed. You're showing signs of consistency and responsibility. They may be waiting for the expected reversion to "old behavior", but when it doesn't arrive, they're pleasantly surprised. Maybe they decide to give you more time to fail or maybe they start to develop a small degree of what they haven't felt toward you in some time, (dare we say it …) T-R-U-S-T. Better still, are you starting to feel that way about you?

Regaining Trust is about the best goal I can think of as you continue to progress toward Authenticity and **Second-Nature Sobriety.**

With your Relentless Self-Honesty, you'll project an aura of Trustworthiness as you interact with new acquaintances. A modest degree of self-assuredness in your Core Strengths will add to this favorable impression. Caution!...you may be heading toward popularity among humans.

If you still think **"No one will ever know…"**

YOU WILL.

COMMITMENT

"I never put off until tomorrow what I can possibly put off until the day after tomorrow."
- Oscar Wilde

The use of force doesn't create true Commitment. At most, it causes compliance. The use of coercion, temptation, or promises won't do it either. These are Ego-based approaches. A fair amount of time will be spent in search of an escape hatch from any perceived commitment. If you have a lingering doubt, if you're not convinced you need a change in lifestyle, if anything other than *absolute commitment* is brought to the Change Effort, it is virtually guaranteed that a slip or a relapse will occur and the cause will be Flawed Commitment, Inattentive Attitude, or both.

As I expressed earlier, nothing drives your commitment level higher than exercising choice. Freedom, personal empowerment, and self-responsibility are brought into play when choice occurs. In the case of making a commitment to the choice of Sobriety, your former feelings of captivity, powerlessness, and irresponsibility will quickly fade. The likelihood of change having success is heightened as a result.

The sustainability of a commitment stems from the clarity of the choice we've made. That clarity helps keep us on the right path toward our goal and reinforces our personal integrity. I recently learned about an instruction given during a class of potential motorcycle drivers which was, "Don't look where you don't want to go." The same could be said about keeping your Commitment on the right track.

Authentic freedom will occur from genuine commitment to the exercise of Core Strengths. Strong Integrity will keep you on what you know to be your right course of action.

When I think of creating and sustaining a genuine commitment to achieving **SECOND-NATURE SOBRIETY**, there are two phrases (well-intentioned they may be) that will never be part of the process. They are, "Just get back on that horse that threw you." And, my favorite, "Relapse is a part of Recovery."

Ultimately, they each send a message that the approach you're considering, or actually following, is doomed to failure. Don't these phrases serve as endorsements of the Insanity Definition? ... repeating the same behavior and expecting different results.

ETHICS & INTEGRITY

"Be sure you put your feet in the right place, then stand firm."
- Abraham Lincoln

Our Core Strengths are the essence of who we are. They become the foundation for our personal Code of Ethics, the operating manual for living our lives. Integrity is our Performance Record, our moral "report card". Ask yourself, "What's *my* grade?"

If you've really made a choice for, and a commitment to, Foundational Change, you also have to choose and commit to the practice of Integrity. Otherwise, the effort invested only produces temporary results and you know there's no real satisfaction or Happiness in that outcome. In the Weight Loss area, dropping and then regaining those "few extra pounds" is an example of that approach. In the Addiction Recovery area, it's called a "Relapse".

When we choose to engage in behavior that's in sync with our positive Ethics, we experience a sensation of "being in the flow". Things just seem to feel right. You may not be consciously pursuing it, but you probably have a general sense that "everything's right with the world". This is not some Moral Balancing Act you're intentionally performing. It is Second-Nature to you and you're experiencing it *without even thinking about it*. Your Integrity "report card" carries an "A" for living with Authenticity. You're experiencing Happiness for what seems to be no reason, but what's really happening here is as simple as the principle of Cause and Effect.

What happens when we operate with another set of Ethics such as the set that supports addictive behavior? This set of Ethics enables us to pursue manufactured temporary euphoria in order to experience the sense that "everything's right with the world". This actually *is* a Moral Balancing Act and it *is* performed with intention. You're experiencing Pleasure, not Happiness, and you're actually practicing Ignorance as you fail to see the true nature of things. Your Integrity "report card" carries a "D" for deluding your true nature. The principle of Cause and Effect is still at work, but the result is actually the opposite of what you think it is.

Let's look inside the Addict's head. A few minutes ago, the sensation that "everything's right with the world" came along and the experience is described as "getting high". He thinks, "Cool. I want more. Now!" The Mindset at work is Impulse to Action with no Thought between. Getting "high" actually results in getting "low" since you engage contact with lower level traits on the Behavioral scale. The Ethics that are supporting this are the "B" Team and they're really good at producing negative consequences. Now you know why someone with a lot of negative consequences from their behavior is sometimes referred to as a "low life".

"I must have been out of my mind. I don't know what I was thinking. It wasn't me." There's a lot of accuracy in those words, but do you *really* want to see how much longer you can say them or are you ready to change your Ethics? Are you prepared to practice Integrity?

Remember that you have lots of prior experience with practicing Integrity. At times, it was practiced in support of the wrong activity for you and frequently resulted in negative consequences. Now that you're regaining some clarity, you're ready for a new application of your Integrity and it will be guided by the power of **New Thought**.

INTEGRITY & THE LAW OF ATTRACTION

Several years ago, I had the honor of attending a retirement dinner held for a very dear friend of mine named, Paul, who has helped me when I needed it most. He had been a highly regarded professional during his career in public service for a large metropolitan area and the dinner was attended by all of his office associates and many high-profile civic "movers and shakers". Following dinner, there were proclamations read from the City Board of Supervisors, the Mayor, the Governor, and one from a guy named, Kelly, who owned the Irish Pub around the corner from City Hall.

After these formalities, the time had arrived for the speeches. I was expecting nothing more than various forms of "roasting" and, while each speaker *did* engage in that activity, every one of them finished with a common, serious, and consistent theme. Without exception, they each ended with words of praise for Paul's Integrity and the profound influence that had for them in their own careers. I knew that Paul possessed many excellent qualities, but I had never summed them up with the use of the most appropriate word to describe them, Integrity.

Integrity is a behavioral characteristic supporting Authenticity. Integrity is commonly used to describe behavior that consistently adheres to Positive Ethics. It also supports the Law of Attraction. People are naturally drawn to someone who is *authentic* or "real"; someone who lives with Integrity. At the same time, that person draws Authenticity from those they meet as they interact. There is a type of personal magnetism taking place. These are the people in our lives that we "just like being around" and they tend to bring out the best in ourselves.

However, Integrity can also have a negative side if it is practiced in adherence to "questionable" Ethics, i.e. Dishonesty, Envy, Addiction, Greed, etc. Unfortunately, the Law of Attraction still applies in this case and it normally results in negative consequences. Our goal is to eliminate Addiction and make Sobriety one of our Positive Ethics which will eventually mature to the status of Second-Nature.

During the research I conducted for this work, I came across more than a few websites that were repackaging the Law of Attraction as being the "secret" to fame and prosperity and everything else short of a guarantee for winning the Lotto jackpot. One of them even claimed you could use it to get a better parking spot at the Mall! Another offered it as The Key to My Financial Future and it could be mine for only $19.95 plus shipping & handling, but only if I was among the next 10 people to respond. If I *wanted* a Cadillac, all I had to do was *think a Cadillac*!

As I understand The Law of Attraction, it is a principle of living ethically and with integrity that results in either Happiness or Suffering. The Ethics are subject to your Choice and the Integrity is for you to Practice. What these attract into your life totally depends on you and your process of **Thought**.

Achieving Second-Nature Sobriety requires Awareness and Consciousness of **Thought**. It is **Thought** that operates as the engine that powers our Ethics and Integrity and we can increase its effectiveness as we'll see in the next section.

THOUGHT

"It is what a man thinks of himself that really determines his fate."
- Henry David Thoreau

This is the section of the material that I had previously asked you to approach with an open, blank-slate frame of mind. This is where you are asked to leave your cynicism at the door and to put aside your biases, prejudices, and preconceived notions. Remember, "Select the nuggets, not the whole mine".

AM I WHO I THINK I AM?

Have you finally reached the point where you've realized it's time to throw out the cases and cases of Shoulda, Coulda, Woulda and If Only that you've been carting along? Is it time to give the "heave-ho" to the "Yeah, buts" and stop "Excuse-ing" yourself from achieving what you truly want, need, and deserve? If so, it's also time to stop living with daydreams and to start living with reasonable expectations. Where Foundational Change is concerned, your new focus has to be "Progress, not Perfection." Your goal is to achieve *Authenticity through Positive Integrity.* Your Power of Thought is going to drive your Attitude and Behavior to a destination of either Happiness or Suffering. Go ahead...make a Choice.

We all have brain chemistry and that is what affects our thoughts, our feelings, and our actions. Conversely, our thoughts, our feelings, and our actions affect our brain chemistry.

If Thought affects our brain chemistry, then *I just may be who I think I am.* If so, I should try to make sure I'm thinking clearly and that I'm keeping misconceptions out of the process.

.
"Am I who I Think I Am?" As Sarah Palin might say, **"Ya Betcha."**

NEUROPLASTICITY

Neuroplasticity is not a new toy developed by WHAM-O, Inc. like the "Super Ball" or "Silly Putty". It is actually the name describing how the human brain can change itself and it is leading to remarkable discoveries. When you engage in new behavior, learning takes place which is the outcome of the brain creating new neural pathways.

In the book "Creative Recovery", authors Maisel and Raeburn offer the following; "Addiction develops through a series of brain changes that involve the strengthening of new memory connections in various circuits of the brain. Negative changes in your ability to think clearly and to feel authentically eventually follow."

They continue, "There is no single biological, psychological, social, environmental, spiritual, or existential factor than can account for anyone's addiction. These factors weave together, interact, magnify one another, and place one person at lesser risk and another person at greater risk." I think that about covers the topic of what causes addiction, eh?

From the book "Train Your Mind, Change Your Brain" by Sharon Begley, we have the following;
"The brain can adapt, heal, renew itself after trauma, and compensate for disability. Experiments in neuroplasticity have found evidence of this. It is possible to reset our happiness meter, regain the use of limbs disabled by stroke, train the mind to break cycles of depression and O.C.D., and reverse age-related changes in the brain."

Remember that Thought drives Attitude which drives Behavior which drives the Learning process. Through the choice of Abstinence, we engage in the Behavior of responding *unfavorably* to the concept of Addiction and *favorably* to the concept of Sobriety. In the process, we may be causing changes in our brain that are reestablishing connections that have been made dormant from addiction.

I'm starting to see a possible connection between Neuroplasticity and Second-Nature Sobriety.

BUMPING INTO BUDDHA

I can practically hear you thinking, "Here it comes. I knew he was going to sell me on the idea of converting to one thing or another." I can gladly assure you, "that ain't the case."

I'm introducing this info to you after calling attention to Neuroplasticity because that concept from Neuroscience has validated some of the beliefs and concepts of Buddhist practices. This high-level, technically-advanced, Neuroscientific research is about 10 years old and the Buddhist practices are about 2500 years old. It seems the new dog is learning old tricks!

A few years ago, if someone tried to "enlighten" me about Buddhist concepts, my eyes would have glassed over as I invited the "Navel-Gazer" to take a hike. Since then, I've tried to become more open and Universal in my thinking and I've done a lot of reading in an attempt to broaden my own thought behind "Second-Nature Sobriety". In doing so, I kept discovering references to Buddhist concepts. They were blatant in some books or on websites and veiled in Westernized language in others, but I kept "Bumping into Buddha".

My point here is that the concepts associated with Buddhism are worth some exploration. Mindfulness Meditation, Consciousness Training, General Awareness, Authentic Happiness, and many other areas are there for the sharing. Personally, I like the way Buddhists think (there must be a bumper sticker for that), but my secular-self says, "Keep the Religion." I feel the same way toward A.A., but I select the nuggets from both sources, not the whole mine.

As an example, I don't have to declare myself as being a "Buddhist", an "Alcoholic", or an "Addict" in order to practice Mindfulness, Awareness, and Happiness. These are concepts that result in healing, wisdom, and personal freedom. They produce perspective, balance, and revitalization of the Human Spirit. They are Universal in their nature and are produced from Thought.

I'm starting to see a connection with Neuroplasticity, Buddhist Philosophy, and Second-Nature Sobriety.

"All that we are is the result of what we have thought."
- Buddha (563BCE – 483BCE)

THE HUMAN "THERMOSTAT"

I recently learned that Scientific Research has found that people develop an emotional "set-point" during their lives. It represents what we each consider to be our personal average range of emotion; our "comfort zone". The research estimates that 50% of the zone is genetically determined and 50% is learned over time. Most of this "learned" part is determined by Thought. This part is considered to be changeable! We can actually learn how to be happier than we currently think we are!

In her excellent book, "Happy For No Reason", author Marci Shimoff offers, "7 Steps for Being Happy From the Inside Out". My favorite step is "Don't Believe Everything You Think."

How you get to that state of mind ("Happy for No Reason") is through the development of Awareness and Consciousness of your Thought and of the resulting feelings you have toward it. If your perception of reality is out of whack, your reaction to it will be as well. You may actually discover that you've been *unhappy for no reason*.

Addicts engage in mood-altering behavior to seek relief from their self-perception. Now that you have some clarity in your mental process, why not turn up your emotional "thermostat'?

HAPPINESS

"Happiness is the meaning and purpose of life, the whole aim and end of human existence. It is the goal of all goals."
-Aristotle

"Those who seek happiness in pleasure...are as naïve as the child who tries to catch a rainbow and wear it as a coat."

– Dilgo Knyentse Rinpoche

As we develop Mindfulness and Awareness, we begin to experience a change in our Attitude. Through the clarity produced by Abstinence and Right Thought, we begin to see that we may have been confusing Pleasure with Happiness.

Pleasure is a short-term condition that produces a sense of euphoria that can be seductive and potentially addictive. Pleasure feeds our self-centered nature and the production of it easily becomes the target of obsessiveness and compulsion. Achieving a State of Pleasure is about as hard to accomplish as microwaving popcorn.

Achieving Authentic Happiness is more substantive and can develop into a favorable personality trait. It is sustainable through the Law of Attraction. Once experienced, Authentic Happiness is far more desirable and rewarding than manufactured euphoria. It is the result of a moral flow created when our Core Strengths, with Sobriety among them, operate consistently. This is what is at the heart of **Second-Nature Sobriety**. *It is a part of who you are; The* <u>*Authentic*</u> *You.*

Happiness has been described as "An absence of Inner Conflict" and it seems reasonable that Suffering would be described as "A presence of Inner Conflict." Inner Conflict occurs when our behavior is in opposition to one or more of our desired Core Strengths. This describes the outcome of engaging in Addiction when Sobriety is the desired strength.

Authentic Happiness is a result of an internal emotional balance that is arrived at through our understanding of Thought and how our mind functions. It can, in time, become second-nature. We establish that state of mind through the application of Right Thought.

Many of us have gone to great lengths of idiocy, even to the point of fabricating false identities, in order to keep ourselves in our personal Pleasure Palace. It wasn't real and now we know it. Consider taking up residency in the Happiness Hacienda where the rent consists of Authenticity.

Author, Matthieu Ricard, a former molecular biologist, a professional photographer, and a Buddhist monk, describes Happiness as "a deep sense of flourishing that arises from an exceptionally healthy mind. It is an optimal state of being." (I should make you aware that Matthieu is also known as, "the happiest man in the world".)

While Happiness is not normally produced and experienced as the result of a single action or event, Buddhists sometimes describe the sensation as being in a "magic moment". They use the term, "Perfect Happiness".

When the San Francisco Giants triumphed in the 2010 World Series, a Dominican-born member of the team was asked by a reporter to describe what the victory meant for him. The player's response was, "I gotta whole lotta Happy!" Wouldn't you want some of that?

BRAIN-TRAIN and THE WHAT-IFS

That's not the name of a new music group, by the way, but it could be the title of the Marketing Plan to bring Neuroplasticity to the attention of the general public. Do a "Google Search" and see how many sites pop up for the topic of Brain Training.

You may have heard one explanation for Addiction as it being the result of having "mis-wired" brain circuits or something similar. What if that were true? But what if we could intentionally "re-wire" our brain circuitry so that we no longer responded to Addictive Impulses? What if it just required a deeper level of consciousness? Is it possible for us to "re-wire" our brain through brain-training so that it responds *unfavorably* to the allure of our addictive nemesis? Hypnosis doesn't reach the depth of consciousness I'm thinking of here.

In the field of organ transplant, some patients are required to participate in a psychological exam to determine if they have the potential to engage in rehabilitation activity at a level which increases the possibility of a successful transplant by practicing required supportive behavior. If it is determined that "you're eligible and have the capacity to respond favorably" to the proposed organ transplant, the process is undertaken. Do you recall the self-assessment of your Strengths and Improvement Areas from section Three? Do you recall the earlier section headed "Mindsets of Change"? Do you recall the importance of Attitude and Commitment? Doesn't all of that ultimately determine your own "capacity to respond favorably" to Abstinence and Sobriety and *unfavorably* to Addiction?

A recent article in an issue of "National Geographic" presented advancements that are occurring in the fields of bionics and artificial limbs or prosthetics. Scientists, Researchers, and Physicians have been successful in creating devices that capture and respond to brain commands sent to the missing limb which is referred to as a "phantom". The patients report that they are achieving prosthetic movement *"without even thinking about it"*. Admittedly, I am stretching that concept, but what if something similar were applied to Addiction and Sobriety?

Through the choice of Sobriety, we attempt to achieve deactivation of Addiction while re-establishing contact with our Sober Self. By "re-wiring" our brain through Brain Training, we are "transplanting" our former "phantom" Sober Self in the void created by the absence of active Addiction. We then engage in the process of Rehabilitation and the practice of Sobriety. What if more emphasis was placed on brain-training to achieve neuroplasticity during rehabilitation? Ideally, we might eventually practice Sobriety *without even thinking about it* and it becomes **Second-Nature.**

I came across something published almost 100 years ago in 1912 (Where does the time go?) titled, "The Master Key System", by Charles Haanel. Some of his "Keys" include, "All experiences in life result from Attitude", "True Power Comes from Within", and "Our World Within is Governed By Our Mind". He wrote, "Every thought brings into action certain physical tissue, parts of the brain, nerve or muscle. This produces an actual physical change in the construction of the tissue." *This guy was describing Neuroplasticity and Buddhist concepts!*

MEDITATION

Not that long ago, I would react to this word as if fingernails were scraping on a nearby chalkboard. I treated the concept as if it had originated on Mars. I thought I was getting where I wanted to go with everything I was using and didn't need some "fringe" sect of Hipness telling me what I needed. I forgot to tell you that "not that long ago" was the early Sixties.

While I admit that I'm not a frequent practitioner of Meditation, I wanted to include this as a source for you to use or explore to improve the effectiveness of Thought in your life. At least, I've learned enough about it to give it a very high "nugget" rating.

Meditation is a mental practice or discipline that leads to a deeper level of self-knowledge. It can help define direction in life. It helps make us more Mindful and Aware which are both Universal human qualities. (I told you I was getting more Open and Universal in my thinking.)

Buddhists engage in this practice to achieve a state they call "Inner Peace" during which they experience a connection with something Westerners might call "Good Vibrations". They experience a Clarity of Thought as a result of seeing the true nature of things. They pursue and experience Enlightenment. This is why I view Addiction as the pursuit and experience of Ignorance.

SECOND-NATURE SOBRIETY

One of the main reasons I was attracted to the concept of The LifeRing approach to recovery was the opportunity to build my own "recipe" for Sobriety while maintaining a sense of Balance in my life. Conversion was not a necessity and creativity was encouraged. I also liked the Positive Psychological approach at its core. Thank you, Martin Nicholas, for creating it. As the author of "Empowering Your Sober Self", Martin points out, "Whatever helps to grow the sober self leads to recovery. Just reducing the addict self, *without more*, has no effect unless the sober self grows and fills the gap."

He continues, "Addiction has hijacked the person's original self; it has stolen its energies, feelings, thoughts and dreams, its very identity. Recovery gives them back. What we recover when we recover is our original self, the authentic us, the sober person we were meant to be and really are."

By writing *"After the Crisis...*Second-Nature Sobriety", I have tried to explore Mr. Nicholas' concept more deeply and expansively while retaining his original focus. It has been very enlightening and has given me a new appreciation for maintaining Balance in life.

Balance was obviously something I severely lacked when I lived in Addiction Heights. I relied heavily on Impulsive Action with virtually no Thought toward Consequences. When Consequences became apparent, I viewed them with Ignorance and played the

Blame Game. When I finally lost the Blame Game, I realized the vital need for Personal Balance and this is what the approach of **Second-Nature Sobriety** has created for me.

Personal Balance for me does not mean being immune to life's ups and downs or walking a thin line to avoid them. It means developing the ability to experience them with confidence derived from personal authenticity. One core element of my personal authenticity is **Second-Nature Sobriety** and I do not offer the concept as being a cure, but rather, as a change in perspective.

Ultimately, Second-Nature Sobriety is a

<u>FOUNDATIONAL CORRECTION of THOUGHT.</u>

I wish you success as you move forward and hope that you give the content of this work due consideration. I hope that you choose to pursue Authenticity and cease taking the "high" road by taking the High Road. It will only lead to Happiness.

Above all, if you choose Sobriety to be one of your Core Strengths. Make it...

SECOND-NATURE SOBRIETY

"Reality is a crutch for people who can't cope with drugs."

- LilyTomlin

AUTHENTIC YOU

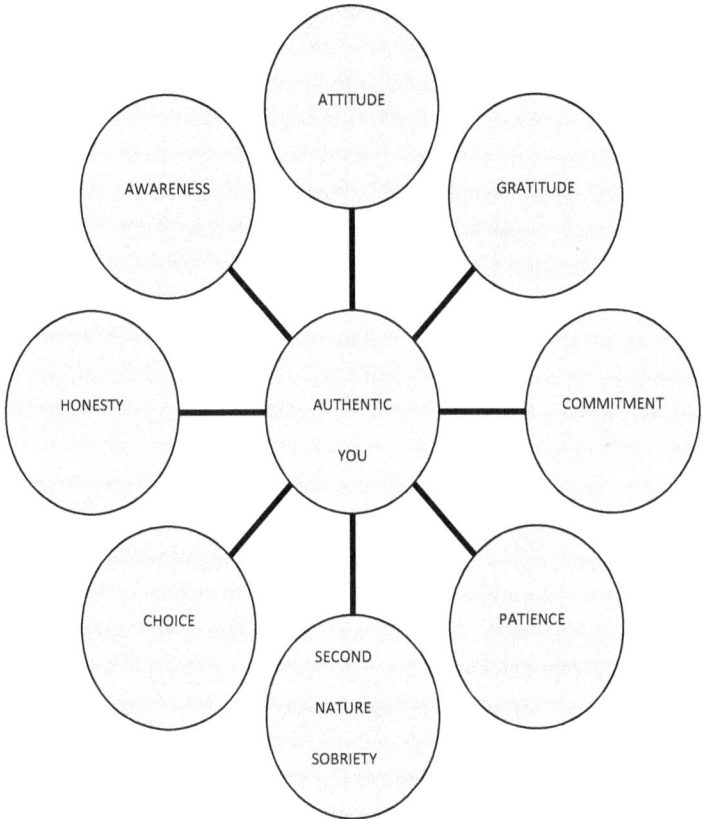

Achieving the "Authentic You" requires the redevelopment of basic trust in ourselves, a sense of self-worth, trust in others, personal growth and understanding, and a sense of healthy shame, vulnerability, and humility. We need to rediscover our ability to make emotional attachments, moral decisions, and exercise Patience.

WHOLE LOTTA HAPPY

"I gotta whole lotta happy!"

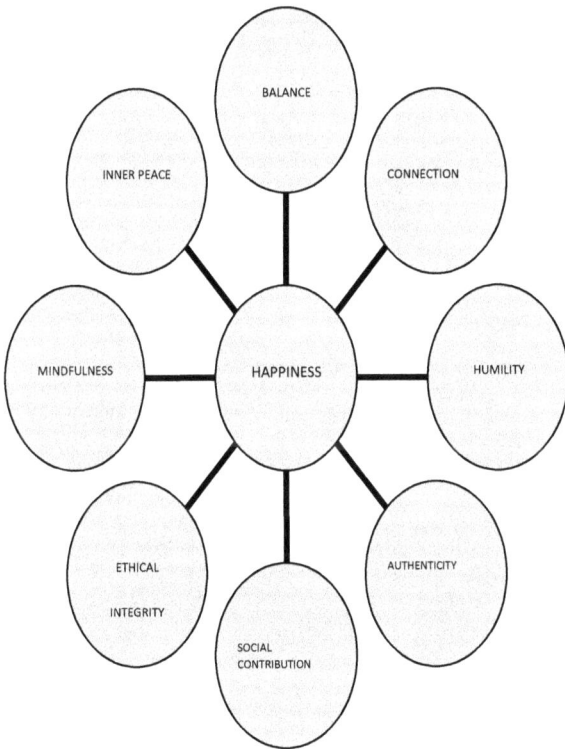

BALANCE

INNER PEACE

CONNECTION

MINDFULNESS

HAPPINESS

HUMILITY

ETHICAL
INTEGRITY

AUTHENTICITY

SOCIAL
CONTRIBUTION

RESOURCES

"Living Deeply: The Art and Science of Transformation in Everyday Life"
                    -Schlitz, Amorok, and Vieten

"Empowering Your Sober Self" – Martin Nicolaus

"Train Your Mind, Change Your Brain"
                    – Sharon Begley

"Creative Recovery" – Maisel and Raeburn

"National Geographic" magazine – January 2010 issue

"Healing the Shame That Binds You"
                    – John Bradshaw

"Six Pillars of Self-Esteem" – Nathaniel Branden, PH.D

"Atlas Shrugged" – Ayn Rand

"Addictive Thinking" – A.J. Twerski, M.D.

"Collective Wisdom and the trap of collective folly"
                    - Briskin, Erickson, Ott, and Callanan

"Under the Influence" – K. Ketcham, J. Milam

"Beyond the Influence" – Ketcham, Asbury, Schulstad, and
                                        Ciaramicoli

"Authentic Happiness" – Martin Seligman, PH.D

"Learned Optimism" – Martin Seligman, PH.D

"Success Principles" – Jack Canfield

"Happy for No Reason" – Marci Shimoff

"Shame: The Power of Caring" – G. Kaufman, PH.D

"The Art of Happiness" – H H Dalai Lama

"The Universe in a Single Atom" – H H Dalai Lama

"The Art of Living Consciously" – Nathaniel Branden, PH.D

"Neuro-Linguistic Programming"
                    - Richard Bandler,   John Grinder

"The Sedona Method" – Hale Dwoskin

"The Power of Self Coaching" – Joseph Luciani, PH.D

"Self-Coaching: How to Heal Anxiety and Depression"
                    – Joseph Luciani, PH.D

"The Quest for Authentic Power" – G. Lawford

"Slaying the Dragon" – William L. White

"Facing Shame" – Fossum and Mason

"Transactional Analysis" (NLP) – Eric Berne, M.D.

"The Answers Within" – Lankton

"Creative Aggression" – Bach and Goldberg

"Internal Dialogue" – Ellis and Beck

"Freedom from Addiction" – Simon and Chopra

"The Motivating Function of Thinking about the Future:
 Expectations Versus Fantasies"
                                    - G. Oettingen, D. Mayer

"12 Stupid Things That Mess Up Recovery"
                        – A. Berger, PH.D

"Illuminating the Shadow: An Interview with
Connie Zweig" – S. London

"All About Responsibility" – N. Branden, PH.D

"Reflections on Happiness" – N. Branden, PH.D

"Reflections on the Ethics of Selflessness"
                        – N. Branden, PH.D

"Stumbling on Happiness" – D. Gilbert

"Kinds of Minds: Toward an Understanding of
Consciousness" – D. Dennett

"Transtheoretical Model of Change (TTM)"
                        – Prochaska and DiClemente

"REBT" – A. Ellis. PH.D

"Three Minute Therapy" – M.R. Edelstein, PH.D

"Nuerogenesis of the Human Brain: Fact or
Fiction" – S Wall.

"Buddha's Brain" – Rick Hanson, PH.D

Websites

AuthenticHappiness.com

Unhooked.com

LifeRing.com.

IONS.com

Stressgroup.com.

Psychcentral.com

Happyfornoreason.com

Transformationalleadershipcouncil.com

TED.com - Matthieu Ricard

Cindysense.com - 21 Habits of Happy People

Sedona. com

HolisticHappiness.com

Mysoberlife .com

Meetings

LifeRing

Alcoholics Anonymous

www.ingramcontent.com/pod-product-compliance
Lightning Source LLC
Chambersburg PA
CBHW071018040426
42443CB00007B/832